Making Paper

by Sarah Allen

illustrated by Chris Evans

Cambridge University Press

Cambridge

London   New York   New Rochelle

Melbourne   Sydney

Paper is all around us every day,
from wallpaper and paper lampshades
to the tissues you blow your nose on.
Many kinds of food are wrapped in paper –
such as biscuits, fish fingers, flour and sugar.
Pound notes are made of paper.

Vast quantities of paper are used to print
words and pictures on – in books,
magazines and newspapers.
The paper this book is printed on was made
in the way described in the book.

3

Most paper is made of wood, and the wood comes from many different kinds of tree, such as spruce, beech and pine.

Some forests are grown especially to be made into paper.
Foresters make sure that trees are planted to take the place of the ones that are cut down.
After the trees have been cut down, they are stripped of their bark.

Then some of the logs are fed into
a huge grinder, which revolves and
grinds them to wood pulp.
This sort of pulp is called *mechanical*.
It is used to make coarse paper of the kind
used for newspaper, which turns yellow after
a while.

To make better quality paper, other logs are
chopped up into chips and mixed with
chemicals and lots of water, to break
down the wood into fibres.
Surprisingly, this pulp is called *wood-free*!

The liquid pulp mixture goes in at one end of an enormous machine, and finished paper comes out of the other end.
First the pulp mixture is poured over a wire mesh sheet, which can be 3 to 7 metres (10 to 23 feet) wide, and moves quickly over a series of rollers.

This is called the *wet end* of the machine because at this stage the mixture is 99% water. The water begins to drain through the mesh, leaving a thin layer of very wet pulp.

The sheet of wet pulp on the wire now
moves over suction boxes which suck out
a lot more of the water.
If you hold a sheet of paper up to the light
you may see the *water mark* design.
This is pressed into the pulp by a wire mesh
cylinder, called the *dandy* roll.

Then the sheet of pulp passes onto a felt band
and goes round a series of up to 100
enormous heated rollers.
Now it starts to look like paper.

It has to be tested for holes.
The hole detector machine passes a beam of
light across the paper.
If there is a hole, the beam shines through.
The machine minder marks the edge of the
paper so that the section can be taken out later.

Working the computerised hole detector

Before it is *sized* all paper is like blotting paper.
It must be coated with a chemical mixture
to make it less absorbent.
The sized sheet goes through more heated
rollers and is then scanned by the computer to
check its thickness and how much water it contains.

If a very smooth, extra-white paper is needed,
it goes through more heated rollers and
is coated with a mixture of chalk, or
china clay, and water.
A small roller with a blade scrapes it
to give a smooth surface.

13

Heated
rollers

Small roller
with blade

Now the paper is wound onto enormous reels.
If the paper accidentally breaks, the machine
stops, and the machine minder winds the
paper back onto the reel and marks the break.

All the reels have to be rewound to get the
side edges straight, and at this stage the
torn edges are trimmed straight and
stuck together with thin tape.

Before they are sent out from
the paper mill, each reel is
wrapped in waterproof brown paper
or plastic, and labelled so that
everyone knows what sort of
paper it is.
Some paper is cut into
sheets instead of being
put on a reel, and this is
also wrapped.

All waste paper in the
paper mill is re-used.
Large pieces are cut up by
a *guillotine*.
Then it is all sent up a
conveyor belt to the
pulper to be broken down into
pulp and *recycled*.

Old, used paper can be processed
all over again to make recycled paper.
Some charities and youth groups collect
waste paper and sell it to firms which sort it
and then take away lorry loads of it to the paper mills.
Most waste paper has been printed or written on.
Before it can be pulped, the ink has to be
removed by treating it with chemicals.

Although trees are being planted as fast as
they are being cut down, our need for
paper keeps increasing, and recycled paper
has become more important.
We hope that the re-use of waste paper will
give the forests time to catch up.

There are things you can do with waste paper
at home too, like making things out of *papier mâché*.
This is a sort of modelling, using scrap paper
and paste.
First tear the paper into small pieces
and put them in a bowl of water.
When they are very wet, squeeze them out,
throw away the water and add some
wallpaper paste to the wet paper.
Mix this up with a little water until
it's mushy and sticky.

You can make all sorts of shapes with the sticky
lumps of paper: bowls, masks, puppet heads.
To finish off the shape, lay pieces of paper
smoothly over the shape one at a time and
paint paste on top.
Put the finished mould in a warm place to dry.
After about a week you can paint and varnish it.

The very first paper was made in China, from silk, and paper can be made from cotton rags and many types of plant.

Some people enjoy making their own paper at home. They may add leaves or petals to their pulp mixture, to make the finished paper look more interesting. Home-made paper can be made from scrap paper, but people use rags or plants as well.

china clay	fine, white clay, also used for making porcelain
guillotine	machine for cutting paper
machine minder	person who looks after a machine
mesh	net or grid
size	give paper a surface that can easily be written or printed on

The author and illustrator would like to thank the East Lancashire Paper Mill Company and Bowaters UK Paper Ltd for their help in the research for this book.